Yankee Whalers

by M. J. Cosson

Content Advisor:
Richard J. Bell
History Department
Harvard University

Rourke
Publishing LLC
Vero Beach, Florida 32964

www.rourkepublishing.com

Image Credits:
Library of Congress, cover (top right and bottom right), 1, 4, 6-7, 9, 10, 11, 12, 13, 15, 16, 17, 19, 20 (right), 21, 22 -23, 24, 25, 26 (right), 28, 29, 30, 31, 33, 34, 38, 40, 44 (bottom), 45 (top and middle), 46; North Wind Picture Archives, cover (top left), 14, 37, 39; Stock Montage 20, 44 (top); iStockphoto 5, 26 (left), 27, 35, 36, 42, 43

Editorial Direction: Red Line Editorial, Inc.; Bob Temple

Editor: Nadia Higgins

Designer: Lindaanne Donohoe

Fact Research: Laurie Kahn

Library of Congress Cataloging-in-Publication Data

Cosson, M. J.
  Yankee whalers / by M.J. Cosson.
    p. cm.— (Events in American history)
  ISBN 1–60044–140–8 (hardcover)
  ISBN 978-1-60044-360-2 (paperback)
  1. Whaling—New England—History—Juvenile literature. I. Title.

  SH383.2C67 2007
  639.2'80974—dc22

                                    2006018912

Printed in the USA

Rourke
Publishing LLC
Vero Beach, Florida 32964

Table of Contents

Chapter One

The Hunt

"There blows! There blows!" the lookouts yelled as the whale leaped out of the water. The captain ran to look through the spyglass. "Ready the boats!" the captain called. The hunt was on!

It was the 1850s, and Yankee whalers dominated the world's whaling industry. Their ships left New England ports in search of whales thousands of miles away. Whale oil and parts were prized for many uses. The whalers were determined to catch the valuable animal.

The mate, the harpooner, and four rowers jumped into the whaleboat as it was lowered to the sea. Other whaleboats followed. The boats could chase the whale for up to four hours.

Whale oil was used for lighting lamps, to make perfume and soap, and to finish leather and woolen products.

Old whaling harpoons

The Right Whale

The right whale was so called because it was the "right" whale to catch. It was the first whale Yankee whalers hunted. The right whale is large and slow moving, and it stays close to shore. An adult right whale is generally 45 to 65 feet (13.7 to 19.8 meters) long and weighs from 70,000 to 200,000 pounds (31,751 to 90,718 kilograms). It could yield 90 barrels of oil.

The right whale also provided valuable baleen plates, which were used to make springs for sofas and carriages, horse-whips, and other products. Baleen plates are inside the whale's mouth. The plates are made of keratin, the same substance that fingernails are made of. They work like a strainer to trap food inside the whale's mouth. As the whale swims along with its mouth open, it gathers water full of tiny sea animals. It closes its mouth and uses it tongue to press out the water through 400 to 540 baleen plates.

A right whale has a round, dark body with white patches on its belly. The white patches are parasites, which are tiny sea creatures that live off the whale's body.

When a whaleboat closed in on its target, the harpooner stood and took aim. His harpoon was barbed like a fishhook so it would stay inside the whale's flesh. Rope was attached to one end of the long spear. The other end was attached to the whaleboat.

No one moved or spoke.

"Strike now!" the mate called out. The harpooner stabbed the whale with one harpoon and then another. The crew backed the boat off the whale as it thrashed about in pain.

In this 1850 illustration, a harpooner stands ready to strike a whale from a small boat. Once a whale was killed, it was brought back to the whaleship (shown in the distance) and processed.

At this point, the wounded whale would try to swim away. The crew hung on tight as the whale pulled the boat around. The giant creature would eventually wear itself out.

Sometimes the whale took a whaleboat for a "Nantucket sleigh ride." This was similar to flying along in a speedboat. If the whale dived, it could take the boat down deep with it—and the crew would drown.

When the whale was tired, the whaleboat came alongside. The mate hurled a sharp, pointed spear, called a lance, deep into the whale's body. This made the final kill. Blood shot high overhead from the whale's blowhole. The blood often covered the crew. The whale bellowed, vomited its stomach contents, and died.

"The speed at which he went made it appear as if a gale of wind was blowing and we flew along the sea surface, leaping from crest to crest of the waves with an incessant succession of cracks like pistol-shots. The flying spray drenched us and prevented us from seeing him."

Whaler Frank Bullen, describing a Nantucket sleigh ride

"As I looked he spouted, and the vapour was red with his blood."

Whaler Frank Bullen, describing the death of a whale

Once the whale was dead, the crew hacked a hole in its tail and attached a towrope. They rowed toward the ship, the whale behind them.

When the boats reached the ship, the crew wrapped a chain around the whale's body to secure it. Now, harder work lay ahead.

The mates would cut a large hole in the whale, just above a fin. A man then jumped into the hole and inserted a huge hook. This was a dangerous job for several reasons. First, the whale's body was wet and slippery, which made it hard to handle. And the blood from the whale attracted sharks. If a man lost his balance and fell into the ocean, he would probably be attacked.

The next job was to cut up the whale. Crewmembers pulled on the chain that led from the hook in the whale's body. While the whale hung in the air, men went to work hacking through the skin and blubber, or fat, behind the head. The whale's body rolled over as the first layer of blubber peeled off. The blubber was brought on deck, where crewmembers worked on hacking it into smaller chunks.

The crew tossed the blubber into heated iron pots. The fat sizzled and popped like frying bacon as the oil oozed out. The crew waded about in slippery blubber and blood as they continued to cut up the whale for the steaming pots.

As the oil cooked out of the blubber, the remains would float to the top of the pot. These chunks of crisp, brown fat were called scraps. Crewmembers often nibbled on them as they worked.

Cutting up and boiling the whale's flesh took about three days, after which the huge body was cast adrift. In the meantime, the lookouts continued the watch for another whale. The ship would not head for home until it held all the oil it could carry. It wasn't unusual for a whaleship to stay at sea for two to four years. One ship stayed at sea for eleven years before having enough whale oil to come home.

A whaling ship often returned to port after two or more years at sea.

Chapter Two

Early Yankee Whaling

From the beginning of time, people have harvested whales that washed up onshore. About 2,000 years ago, American Indians started using lookout towers. When a whale was spotted offshore, men in small boats would chase it.

In 1620, Pilgrims sailing from England to America noted "hordes of whales in the coastal waters." Their ship, the *Mayflower*, was likely used as a whaleship before it made its journey to the New World.

The Mayflower

"Our plot was there to take Whales for which we had [several] ... experts. ... We found this Whale-fishing a costly conclusion; we saw many and spent much time in chasing them, but could not kill any."

English adventurer John Smith, who made the first whaling voyage to New England, arriving off the coast of Maine in 1614

Yankee whaling refers to whaling from New England towns along the northeast coast of the United States. It started toward the end of the seventeenth century with a group of Christians called Quakers. Quakers held some different beliefs than other Christians, such as refusing to fight in a war. They came to America from England, where they had been mistreated for their differences.

Quakers worship at loosely organized "meetings," where any member is free to speak out about any issue.

In America, the mistreatment continued. In 1659, a group of Quakers needed to escape from the English settlers on mainland Massachusetts. The Quakers moved to the barren, sandy island of Nantucket. The soil on the island was too poor for farming. As if on cue, a right whale swam into the harbor and died. Soon the Nantucket Quakers had become whalers.

When they had killed off the whales near shore, the Quakers began hunting farther out to sea. They sailed north near Newfoundland, off the east coast of Canada, and to Greenland. In those early whaling trips, the blubber was not boiled on board. It was stored raw in barrels until it could be processed onshore. This made for a poorer quality of whale oil.

An old map showing Massachusetts amd surrounding states along the Atlantic Ocean

The Sperm Whale

The sperm whale can be 36 to 60 feet (11 to 18 meters) long and can weigh from 30,000 to 90,000 pounds (13,608 to 40,823 kilograms). Whalers could tell they were chasing a sperm whale because it has one blowhole rather than the two blowholes baleen whales have.

The sperm whale produces spermaceti, a very high quality oil that comes from a large cavity (the "case") inside the whale's head. Also in the head is the "junk," which is much like a sponge filled with spermaceti. The sperm whale is the only whale to produce ambergris, a gray, waxy substance found in the intestines. Ambergris was used to make perfume and was the most valuable product from a whale. It was as expensive as gold.

Whalers also harvested the sperm whale's jaw and removed the teeth so that crewmembers could carve them into beautiful scrimshaw. Sperm whales have teeth only in the lower jaw. The use of the teeth is not known, but they possibly could be used to help sperm whales grab and hold on to slippery squid, a favorite meal.

In 1712, Captain Christopher Hussey and his crew got caught in a storm and were blown out to sea. The next day, they spotted a school of whales swimming a short distance away. They hunted and killed the first recorded sperm whale. Whalers soon learned that sperm whales provided a large quantity of high-quality oil. The whales swam where the water was at least 650 feet (198 meters) deep, and they traveled in herds. Soon ships were fitted with equipment so they didn't have to return to shore to render the blubber into oil.

A sperm whale

Whaling took off in 1733, when the British government passed a law promising a bounty, or reward, for each whale that was caught by British whalers. At that time, the United States of America did not yet exist. It was still just a group of colonies ruled by Great Britain. So Britain's laws applied to American colonists as well. By 1749, American whaling had become a powerful part of colonial trade.

In 1765, Joseph Rotch, a Nantucket whaling merchant, built the town of New Bedford, Massachusetts. In time New Bedford would overtake Nantucket as the whaling capital.

In 1762, Nantucket had 78 whaleships. By 1775, it had 150.

Residents of Nantucket dressed up for a visit to the town's wharf, or pier, where whaling ships docked and unloaded their cargo.

Chapter 3

Whaling During the Revolutionary War

In the spring of 1775, fighting broke out between British troops and American colonists. The Americans were fed up with living under British rule. They wanted to form a nation of their own. For the next eight years, the Revolutionary War raged across New England.

The first battles of the Revolutionary War were fought in Massachusetts by American militiamen. These soldiers were ordinary townspeople who trained in their spare time and often supplied their own weapons.

Yankee whalers were affected by the war in many ways. Most were Quakers, so they did not fight in the war. Nevertheless, war found them.

In December 1773, two whaling ships were part of the Boston Tea Party, one of the key events that led to the war. The Boston Tea Party was not a party at all—it was an act of protest against the British government by a group of angry American colonists.

The Americans were outraged by a British law, called the Tea Act of 1773, that allowed the British East India Company to sell tea in the colonies at a cheap price. Colonial merchants could not afford to sell their tea at a similarly low price. They feared customers would buy the cheaper British tea instead of theirs. So colonial leaders came up with a plan to fight the Tea Act.

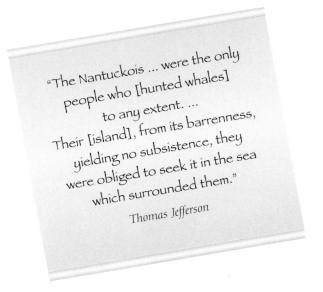

"The Nantuckois ... were the only people who [hunted whales] to any extent. ... Their [island], from its barrenness, yielding no subsistence, they were obliged to seek it in the sea which surrounded them."

Thomas Jefferson

During the Boston Tea Party, angry colonists disguised themselves as
Indians and dumped British tea into the Boston Harbor.

Whaler Crispus Attucks and the Boston Massacre

Crispus Attucks was a seaman and whaler. Some reports say he was of African descent and other reports describe him as American Indian. In 1750, he ran away from his master and went to sea on a whaleship. While on a break from whaling, he met Samuel Adams, the Revolutionary activist. Attucks began to attend meetings of American rebels. After one meeting, on March 5, 1770, British soldiers told a group of colonists to disperse, and the colonists disobeyed. Words were exchanged. The colonists threw snowballs at the British soldiers, who fired shots into the crowd. Five people were killed, including Attucks. On March 5 of every year after that, Samuel Adams published a pamphlet calling the incident the Boston Massacre. Crispus Attucks became a hero, known as one of the first Americans to die for his nation's liberty.

John Hancock participated in the Boston Tea Party.

After the Yankee whaleships *Beaver* and *Dartmouth* had dropped off whale oil in London, the British East India Company hired them to carry tea back to Boston. When these and two other boats came into Boston Harbor, John Hancock, Samuel Adams, and about 200 other American rebels snuck on board. Dressed as American Indians, the group dumped the tea into the ocean. The rebels let the British know that the colonists would not buy their cheap tea.

In October 1775, some six months after the first battles and nearly two years after the Boston Tea Party, the Americans established the Continental Navy to fight the war at sea. Both the American and British forces captured whaleships to use in the war. They made some whalers join their navies.

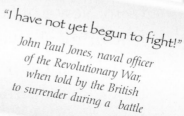
"I have not yet begun to fight!"
John Paul Jones, naval officer of the Revolutionary War, when told by the British to surrender during a battle

Whalers sometimes went on to serve in the U.S. Navy. Here, an officer of the Navy addresses fellow officers aboard a ship.

Two months later, Britain's King George III closed the American colonies to all trade, to take effect on March 1, 1776. It was becoming impossible to go whaling from New England.

During the years 1777 and 1778, Nantucket was blockaded by the British. Yankee whalers could no longer sail from or into the island. Then, in September of 1778, 2,000 British raiders marched to New Bedford, where they burned the town and all the ships in the dock.

King George III

After the Revolutionary War, many Yankee whalers operated from Nova Scotia, Canada. An aerial view of Nova Scotia's harbor shows dozens of ships coming and going.

After the war, conditions didn't get easier. Although they'd lost, the British tried to get back at the Americans by placing a high tax on all Yankee whale products coming into Great Britain. The tax made selling whale products to England out of the question. Yankee whalers had lost valuable customers.

Because the tax applied only to *American* products, Nantucket tried to get around it by declaring itself a separate country. But only 5,000 people lived on the island, so it was an impractical move. Many Yankee whalers moved to Nova Scotia, Canada, to avoid paying the tax. Most of the Yankee whalers, however, remained loyal to New England. Eventually, most of the people went back.

During the 1790s, products from sperm whale oil were in great demand. Yankee whaling ports began to rebound.

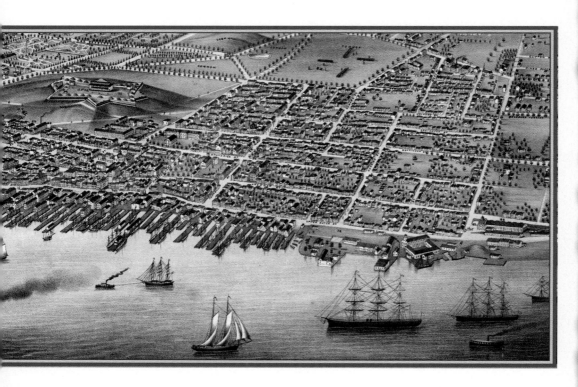

Chapter Four

The Golden Age of Whaling

In 1807, President Thomas Jefferson created the Embargo Act to keep American ships from going to foreign ports. Then, five years later, another war with the British broke out. Like the Revolutionary War, the War of 1812 hurt the whaling industry, which had already been weakened by the Embargo Act. By 1815, though, the golden age of whaling was in full force. The United States dominated whaling for the next 50 years. At least 15 whaling ports thrived up and down the New England coast.

In this political cartoon from 1808, Thomas Jefferson (behind the desk) defends the unpopular Embargo Act to a group of unhappy citizens. The Embargo Act hurt whaling and other industries in the early 1800s.

Between 1785 and 1810 a new type of whaleman was working on ships: the whaler-sealer, who hunted seals as well as whales. Sealskins were traded with Chinese merchants for silks and teas. Whaler-sealers made a number of discoveries that updated and improved maps of the world.

During this golden age, Yankee whalers traveled farther and farther away. Soon they were traveling around Cape Horn, the southern tip of South America, and into the Pacific Ocean.

Sealers killed the Steller's sea cow, ate the meat, drank the oil, and used the thick skin to repair their boats. The last known Steller's sea cow was killed in 1768. In less than 30 years of contact with humans, the Steller's sea cow had become extinct.

Right: Yankee whalers had to travel all the way around South America to get to Hawaii.
Below: Whaler-sealers hunted seals such as the one shown here.

The Hawaiian Islands made a much welcome stop for Yankee whalers hunting in the Pacific. There they obtained fresh water, fruit, vegetables, and hogs. They enjoyed the beautiful scenery and the welcoming friendliness of the Hawaiian people.

Hawaii soon became more than just a stop. The whalers began to deliver their oil and bones to Hawaii. The whale products would then be carried back to the mainland on merchant ships.

In 1774, there were 360 Yankee whaleships. By 1846, there were 735.

Sea-weary whalers welcomed the sight of Hawaii's beautiful shores.

After 1849, many sailors left whaleships to mine for gold in California.

Despite Hawaii's appeal, gold fever soon overtook many of the whalers working in the Pacific. When gold was discovered in California in 1849, these whalers were lured by the promise of riches. They were adventuresome. They were hard workers. They also knew they wouldn't get rich working on a whaleship. By 1852, many whalers had gone to California in search of gold.

In 1859, the discovery of crude oil, or petroleum, in Pennsylvania also sparked the interest of Yankee whalers. They saw another opportunity to make a profit in oil. So that same year, several New Bedford merchants who had been in the whaling industry built a factory to process petroleum.

By 1861, the issue of slavery had split the United States in two. The slave-owning states in the South broke away to form a separate country, the Confederate States of America. For four years, the Northern states, including New England, battled the Southern states during the Civil War.

The Battle of Bull Run, in nothern Virginia, was one of the Civil War's bloodiest.

Frederick Douglass, Black Activist of the Nineteenth Century

Frederick Douglass was a runaway slave from Maryland who devoted his life to ending slavery. Throughout his life, he was helped by whaling in several ways.

Douglass was a gifted speaker. He gave his first speech at the Massachusetts Anti-Slavery Society's convention in Nantucket in 1841. He told how his master's wife had taught him to read because she didn't know that it was illegal for slaves to read. Eventually his master hired him out as a ship caulker in Baltimore. There he met a free black sailor named Benny. In 1838, Douglass escaped by putting on Benny's sailor suit and using his "protection papers" to board a train. He arrived in New York without being caught. Douglass moved to New Bedford, Massachusetts, where a Quaker friend got him a job caulking whaleships.

Douglass became a member of the Anti-Slavery Society. He had to flee to England to keep from being captured. Friends bought his freedom, and he returned to New York. In 1847 he began a newspaper, the *North Star*, dedicated to freedom, justice, and equal rights for all.

The whalers found themselves mixed up in yet another national crisis. For many years, whaling had played a large part in bringing slaves from Africa to the United States, since whaleships could easily be outfitted as slave ships. Also, by 1808, bringing slaves from overseas was illegal in the United States. Yankee whaleships provided slave-ship captains looking to smuggle slaves into the country a perfect place to hide them.

Whaleships were sometimes used as slave ships, like the one pictured here.

At the same time, whaling was part of the movement to end slavery. The Quakers, who still made up a large portion of whalers, believed it was wrong to keep another human being as a slave. They helped hide many runaway slaves on whaleships. Free blacks became sailors because it was one of the few jobs available to them. During the golden age of whaling, African Americans made up one-quarter of whaling crews. Because Yankee whaleships sailed the world, they contained a mix of races not seen anywhere else at that time.

A poster from the mid-1830s condemns slavery. Many whalers were active in the cause to abolish, or put an end to, the practice of slavery.

During the war, Confederate ships destroyed more than 50 Yankee whaleships. But whaleships also served the North in an important role. Thirty-seven old New Bedford whaleships, nicknamed the Stone Fleet, sailed to Southern harbors, where they were filled with stones. The weight of the stones caused the ships to sink, blocking the harbors so Confederate ships couldn't get through.

Several factors helped end the golden age of Yankee whaling. The discovery of petroleum led to a cheaper fuel that was easier to process. Steel was replacing baleen as springs and other items. As the demand for whale products dropped, so did prices. In 1856, sperm oil was $1.77 per gallon; by 1895, it was $.40 per gallon.

Although whaling continued, the industry was in decline. Whales were becoming hard to find because they had been overhunted. Also, changes in technology were making it harder for the small Yankee ships to compete with whaleships from Norway, Japan, and the Soviet Union.

By the late nineteenth century, the use of whale oil had been replaced with petroleum. However, baleen was still used for hoop skirts and corsets for women. Whalers harvested the baleen from a bowhead whale's mouth, then threw away the rest of the whale.

A music cover from 1864 shows oil wells, barrels, and other symbols of "American Petroleum."

Chapter Five

Life on a Whaleship

Life at sea could get lonely. When two whaleships met at sea, they came alongside each other. Often the captains yelled back and forth. Sometimes they even exchanged crews for a day or two to give the men a change of scenery. Whaling ships generally had crews of 25 to 35 men.

Usually, four crewmembers stood watch for whales, two at the front of the ship and two at the back. Some ships had platforms for lookouts to stand on.

Sailors climbed onto lookout platforms such as this one to scan the seas for whales.

The captain's cabin contained a bed, a washstand, and a table. Some captains even brought their wives and children along. Officers had smaller cabins. The crew slept in the forward section, called the forecastle, below the main deck. The only light in the forecastle came from a small

opening overhead. Crewmembers were not paid a steady rate but instead received a portion of the profits. Shipowners took as much as half of the profits. The captain might get 1/8 or 1/10 of the profits. Regular seamen received 1/150. As an example, the average pay on the *James Maury*, which sailed between 1845 and 1868, worked out to about $.26 a day. Unskilled workers on land earned about $.90 a day. Compared to them, whalers didn't make much money.

Necessary items were for sale onboard the ship. The goods cost two to three times what they were worth on land. The amount was withheld from the buyer's pay. Often items a man bought on ship exceeded his pay. If a crewmember went into debt, he had to sign up for the next trip to work off the debt.

U.S. maritime law required the mate to keep a logbook, or diary. Entries included the ship's position at sea, number of whales caught, and illnesses and injuries among the crew. Such entries helped a ship keep track of where the good hunting fields were. Other items mentioned in the logbooks included mutinies, beatings, accidents, fires, and drownings. Sometimes there were notes on hurricanes, tidal waves, shipwrecks, ships struck by lightning, men falling overboard, hostile natives, and ships crushed by ice.

Whalers make the final kill.

Herman Melville and Moby-Dick

In 1851, Herman Melville's novel *Moby-Dick* (or *The Whale*) was published. The famous work is a whaling adventure based, in part, on the author's life.

Herman Melville was born in 1819 in New York City. His family had been well off, but his father died when Melville was 12, leaving his wife and eight children in poverty. At 19, Melville went to sea. He was 22 in 1841 when the whaleship he had signed on to, the *Acushnet*, left New Bedford, Massachusetts, for the Pacific Ocean. Melville had read the story of the whaleship *Essex* in which a mad whale rammed and sank the ship.

He combined aspects of that and stories of a white whale called Mocha Dick that stalked ships in the Pacific to write Moby-Dick, one of the greatest American novels of all time. Melville wrote several other novels throughout his life, but Moby-Dick is his masterpiece.

Herman Melville, author of Moby-Dick

"The reading of this wondrous story [while on] the landless sea, and so close to the very latitude of the shipwreck, had a surprising effect upon me."

Writer Herman Melville, on reading a well-known whaling story about the Essex

Whalers didn't get to drink much fresh water. They drank "longlick," a mixture of coffee, tea, and molasses. They ate salted meat (pork, beef, or horse). A delicacy was fried whale brains. They ate bean soup and duff (a flour pudding). Sometimes they got fresh fish, turtles, dolphins, or, of course, whale meat.

To keep busy and pass the time, the crew ran drills, washed the deck, and sharpened lances and harpoons. They also repaired the boats, mended sails, told stories, and sang songs. They carved beautiful and complicated designs on whale teeth and bones. Such artwork, called scrimshaw, has come to be a symbol of the age of Yankee whalers.

Between hunts, whalers passed the time with stories and songs.

Chapter Six

The End of Yankee Whaling

By the mid-1880s, ships equipped with harpoon guns were killing whales quickly and efficiently. Explosives inside the harpoon killed the whale. After the whale was dead, air was pumped into it to keep it afloat. Another ship towed it ashore for processing.

A few American whaleships continued working into the early twentieth century. Whaling ports on the East Coast disappeared. San Francisco became a staging ground for whaling in the Arctic and northern Pacific. In 1924, the *Wanderer*, the last traditional whaleship to leave New Bedford, ran aground and was wrecked off the coast of Massachusetts.

In 1857, New Bedford had 329 whaleships. By 1907, it had just 32.

Yankee whaleships mapped the most remote areas of the oceans so thoroughly and accurately that the charts were used by American airplane pilots during World War II.

By the 1960s, people were becoming alarmed at how few whales were left on Earth. The United States, Great Britain, France, Canada, Mexico, and Argentina began calling for cuts in the number of whales hunted. In the 1970s, the same countries asked for a worldwide ban on whale hunting. But Japan, the Soviet Union, Norway, and Iceland continued to hunt whales.

Whalers have killed more than 100,000 humpback whales. Only about 15,000 survive today.

A humpback whale breaches, or leaps, out of the ocean.

Scientists estimate that thousands of years ago there were as many as 4.5 million whales. Only a small fraction remains. The mighty whale still fascinates us. Today tourists "hunt" for whales in a different way, armed with binoculars and cameras. It is a powerful thrill just to watch these mighty creatures of the seas.

A whale watcher searches the horizon for a whale coming up for air.

Biographies

Crispus Attucks (ca. 1723–70)

Attucks was a whaler of African or American Indian descent. Attucks became regarded as a hero when he was killed during the so-called Boston Massacre of 1770. That event, in which British troops fired at unarmed American colonists, was one of several that led to the outbreak of the Revolutionary War.

William Bradford (1823–92)

Bradford was a painter of whaling ships and the arctic seas. His father wanted him to work in the family store, but the store failed because Bradford was busy drawing and painting. At 29, he began painting ships. When England's Queen Victoria saw his work, she ordered a painting. Through the years, Bradford became known for his beautiful paintings of ships sailing the icy seas.

Frederick Douglass (ca. 1817–95)

Douglass was a black leader in the movement to end slavery. Born in Maryland, Douglass was a runaway slave who worked for a time in the whaling town of New Bedford, Massachusetts. Douglass was a gifted speaker and writer. His autobiography, *Narrative of the Life of Frederick Douglass*, was first published in 1845. In 1847, he began an antislavery newspaper, the *North Star*, in Rochester, New York.

John Paul Jones (1747–92)

A famous naval officer of the Revolutionary War, Jones is known today as the father of the U.S. Navy. During the Revolutionary War, Jones distinguished himself with his bravery. In 1776, he sailed into Canso Harbor, Nova Scotia, and burned all the British whaleships and oil there. Though not a whaler himself, he sailed with many Yankee whalers.

Herman Melville (1819–91)

Melville is one of the most respected American authors of all time. His most famous book, *Moby-Dick*, is a whaling adventure. It recounts the hunt by Captain Ahab for Moby Dick, a deadly white whale that was supposedly known to Yankee whalers in the 1800s. Melville himself worked aboard a whaleship and had many adventures at sea that took him all around the world. Several of his other novels were based on his experiences in far-flung places.

Manjiro Nakahama (ca. 1827–98)

Nakahama was a Japanese fisherman who was rescued at sea by Captain William Whitfield of the *John Howland* in 1841. Manjiro stayed on the ship and learned whaling. He changed his name to John Mung or John Manjiro and moved to Fairhaven, Massachusetts. There he attended school and learned English. Eventually he returned to Japan, where he taught English, navigation, and whaling. Manjiro served as an interpreter when the United States and Japan began talks about formal relations in the 1850s.

Timeline

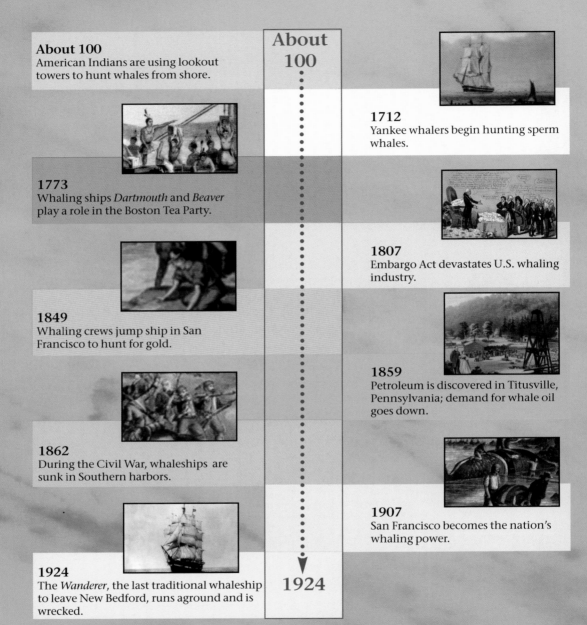

About 100
American Indians are using lookout towers to hunt whales from shore.

About 100

1712
Yankee whalers begin hunting sperm whales.

1773
Whaling ships *Dartmouth* and *Beaver* play a role in the Boston Tea Party.

1807
Embargo Act devastates U.S. whaling industry.

1849
Whaling crews jump ship in San Francisco to hunt for gold.

1859
Petroleum is discovered in Titusville, Pennsylvania; demand for whale oil goes down.

1862
During the Civil War, whaleships are sunk in Southern harbors.

1907
San Francisco becomes the nation's whaling power.

1924
The *Wanderer*, the last traditional whaleship to leave New Bedford, runs aground and is wrecked.

1924

Glossary

ambergris (AM-buhr-grees)
a gray, waxy, crumbly substance found in the intestines of some sperm whales; believed to form around the squid beaks that remain in the whale's stomach; used in making perfume

baleen (buh-LEEN)
flexible, comb-like plates that grow in the mouths of some whales

blockade (blok-AYD)
to block off, or control, who leaves or enters a port or another place

blubber (BLUH-buhr)
thick, oily layer of fat beneath a whale's skin that protects against cold

colony (KOL-uh-nee)
a group of people who settle in a distant land while remaining citizens of their original country; also the word for the place they settle

forecastle (FOR-kas-uhl)
area in the front of the ship where the crew slept

harbor (HAR-buhr)
part of a body of water near a coast in which ships can safely anchor

logbook (LOG-book)
the daily diary in which information of a ship's voyage is recorded

maritime (MAR-uh-tym)
having to do with the sea

mutiny (MYOO-tuh-nee)
rebellion against legal authority by refusing to obey orders and, often, attacking officers, especially aboard a ship

scrimshaw (SKRIM-shaw)
the art of carving on whale teeth, whale bones, and other bones and teeth, such as those of the walrus

Yankee (YAN-kee)
originating from the United States, especially from New England

Further Resources

Web Links

New Bedford Whaling Museum
www.whalingmuseum.org
This site provides a concise history of Yankee whaling, on-line exhibits, a research library, a list of museum events, and information about programs such as the marathon reading of Melville's *Moby-Dick*.

Whale Times
www.whaletimes.org
This site has facts, puzzles, a list of books, and an extensive dictionary of words about whales and whaling.

Books

McKissack, Patricia C., and Fredrick L. McKissack. *Black Hands, White Sails: The Story of African-American Whalers*. Scholastic Press, 1999.

Melville, Herman. *Moby Dick, or, The White Whale*. Retold by Geraldine McCaughrean. Oxford University Press, 1996 (illustrated version of the classic work for young adults).

Philbrick, Nathaniel. *Revenge of the Whale: The True Story of the Whaleship Essex*. G. P. Putnam, 2002.

Index